African Print Inspired Home Decor Coloring Book

Alicia L. McDaniel

Thanks for purchasing our *African Print Inspired Home Decor Coloring Book*. Inspired by the beauty of African textiles and print patterns, this coloring book features a variety of ideas for home decor. Enhance each design by adding patterns, stickers, scrapbook paper and more. Studies show that coloring is a great way to relax and inspire creativity. Visit www.artforthecreativesoul.com to find helpful tips and ideas for coloring this book.

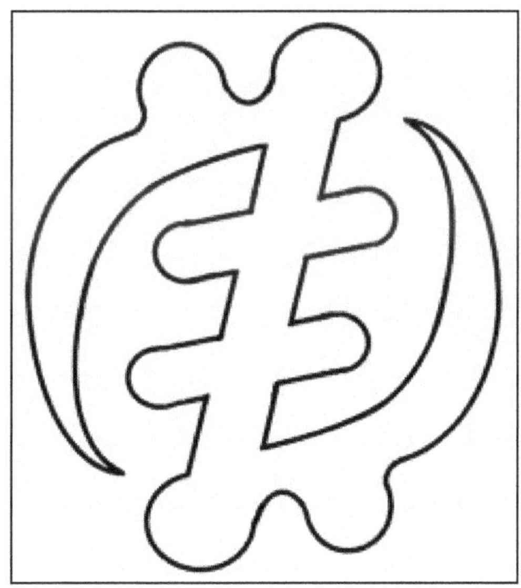

African Print Inspired Home Decor Coloring Book

Published by Alicia McDaniel Fine Art
ISBN: 978-0-9995573-3-4

Thanks for purchasing our African Print Inspired Home Décor Coloring book. These designs are inspired by the beauty of African textiles and print patterns. This coloring book features a variety of designs for home décor. [illegible] design by adding [illegible] stickers [illegible] and more [illegible] show [illegible] [illegible]. Visit [illegible] to find [illegible] [illegible].

African Print Inspired Home Décor Coloring Book
by Allie L. McDaniel © All Rights Reserved
Published by Allie McDaniel [illegible]
ISBN: 978-0-9995573-3-4

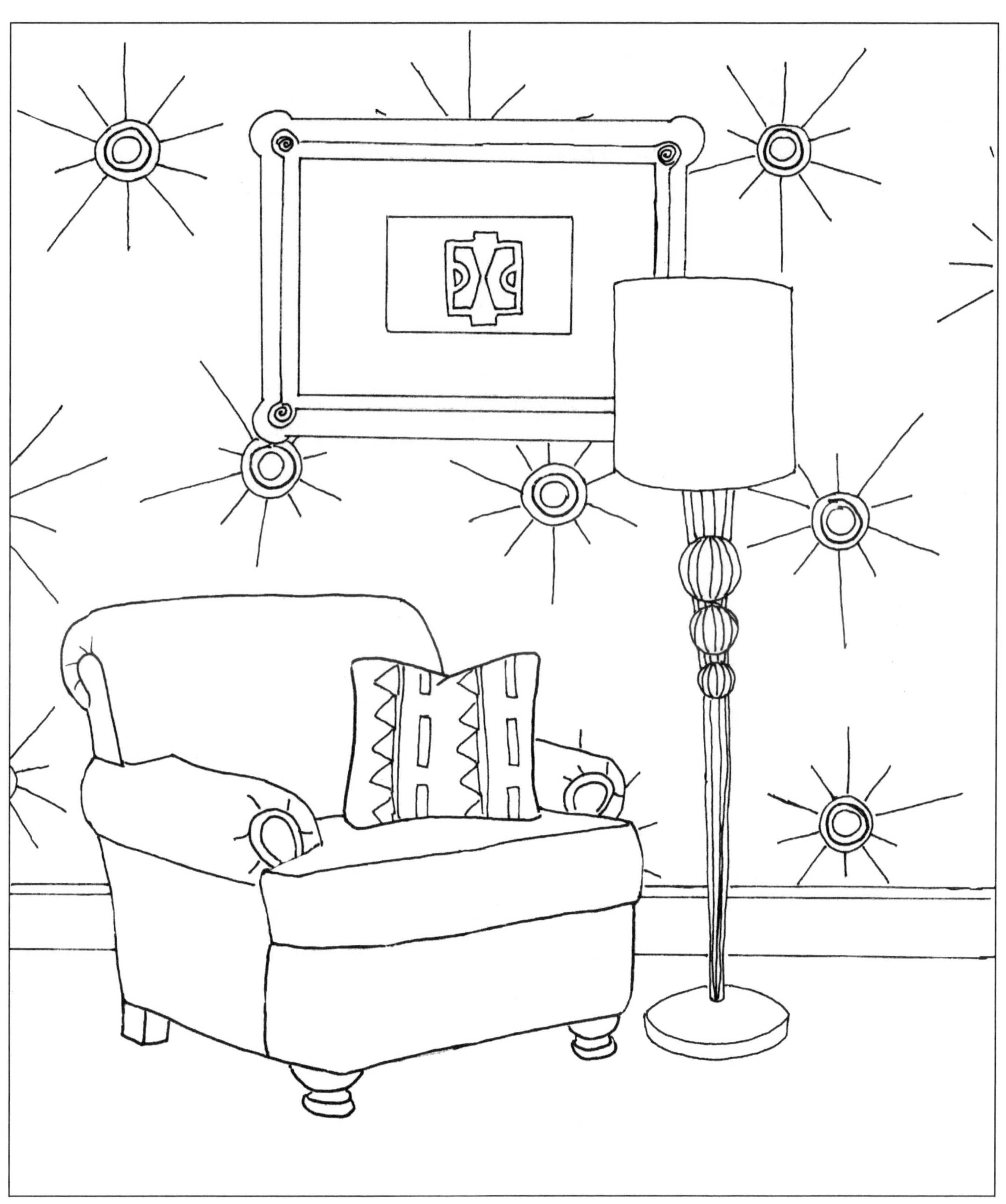

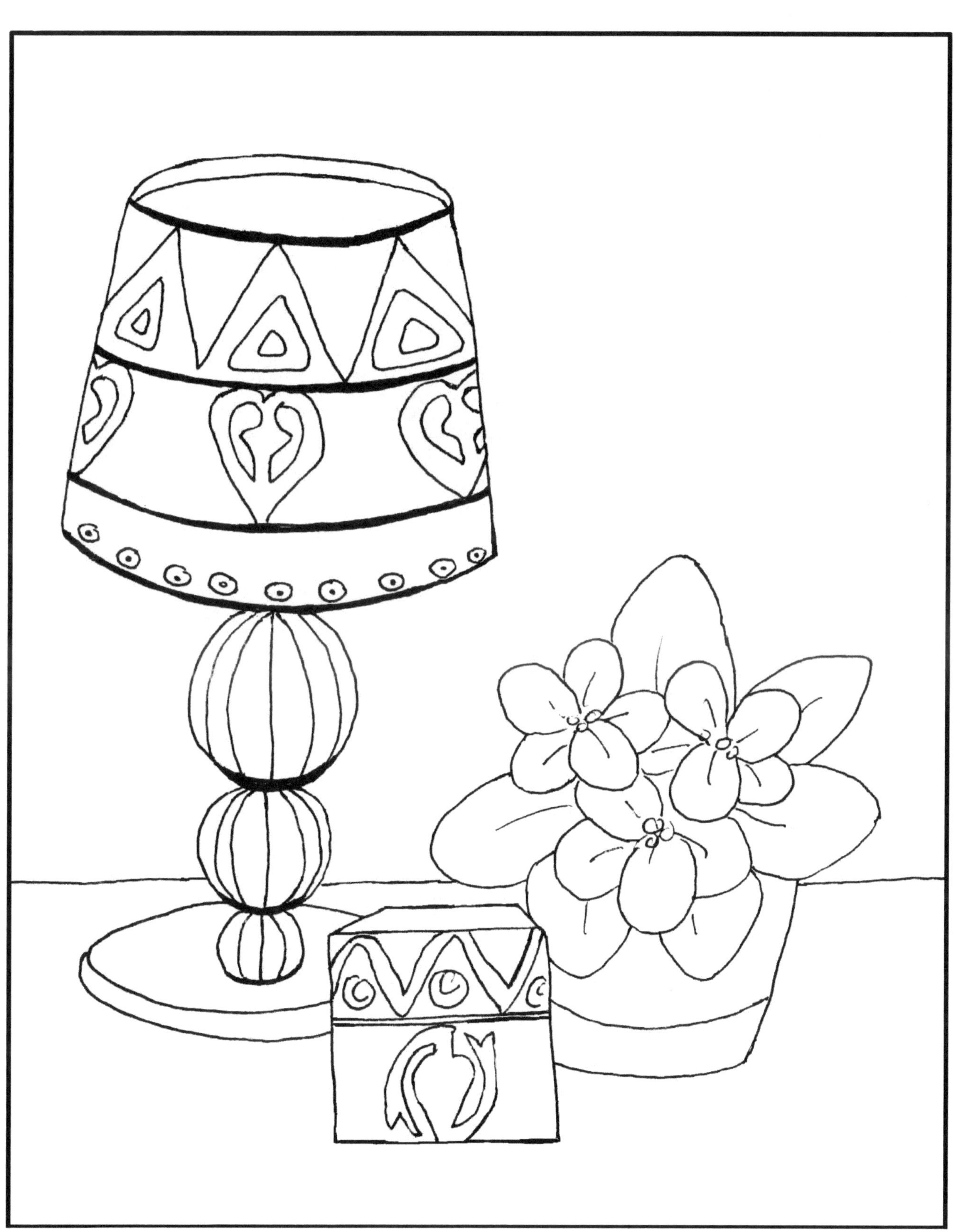

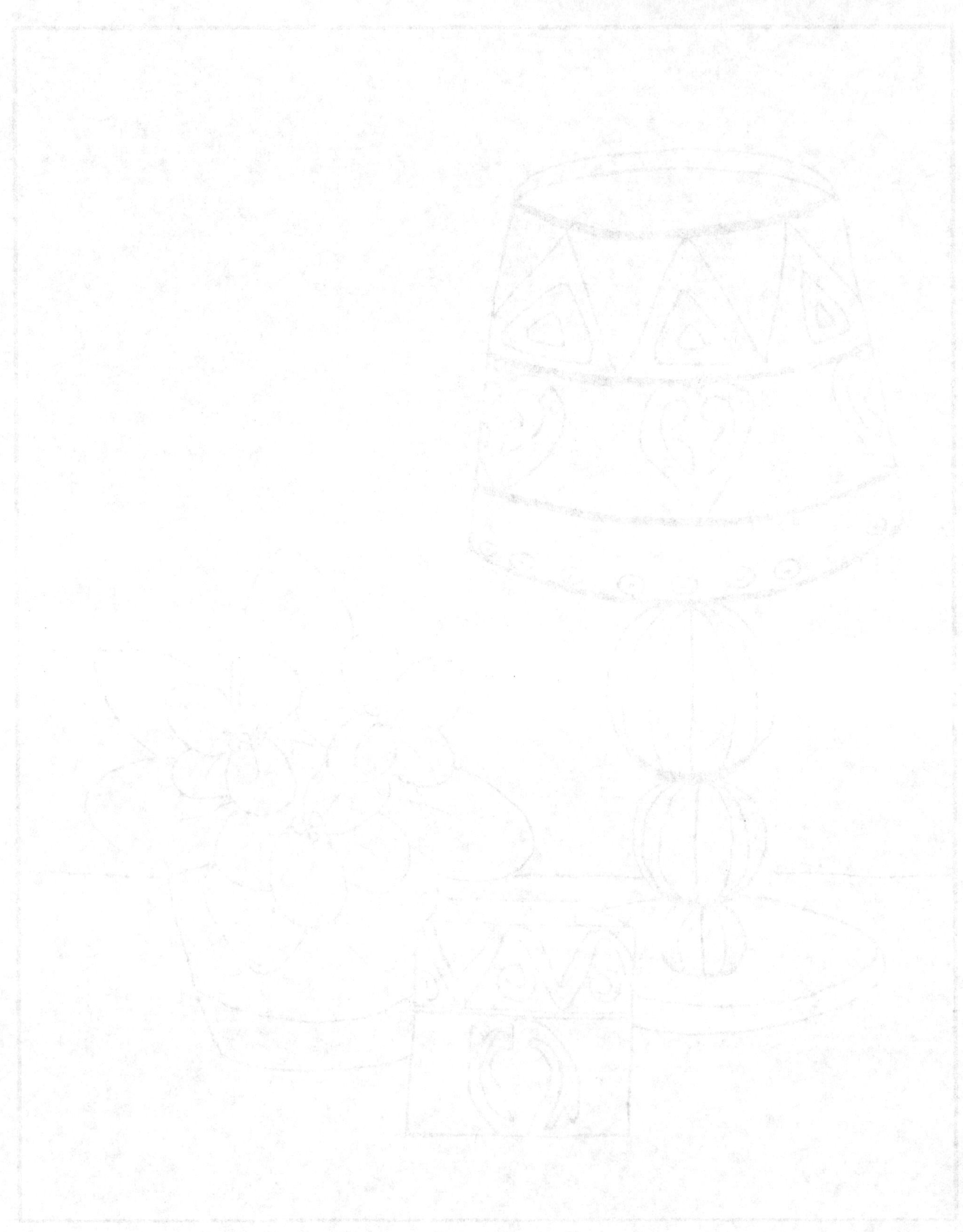

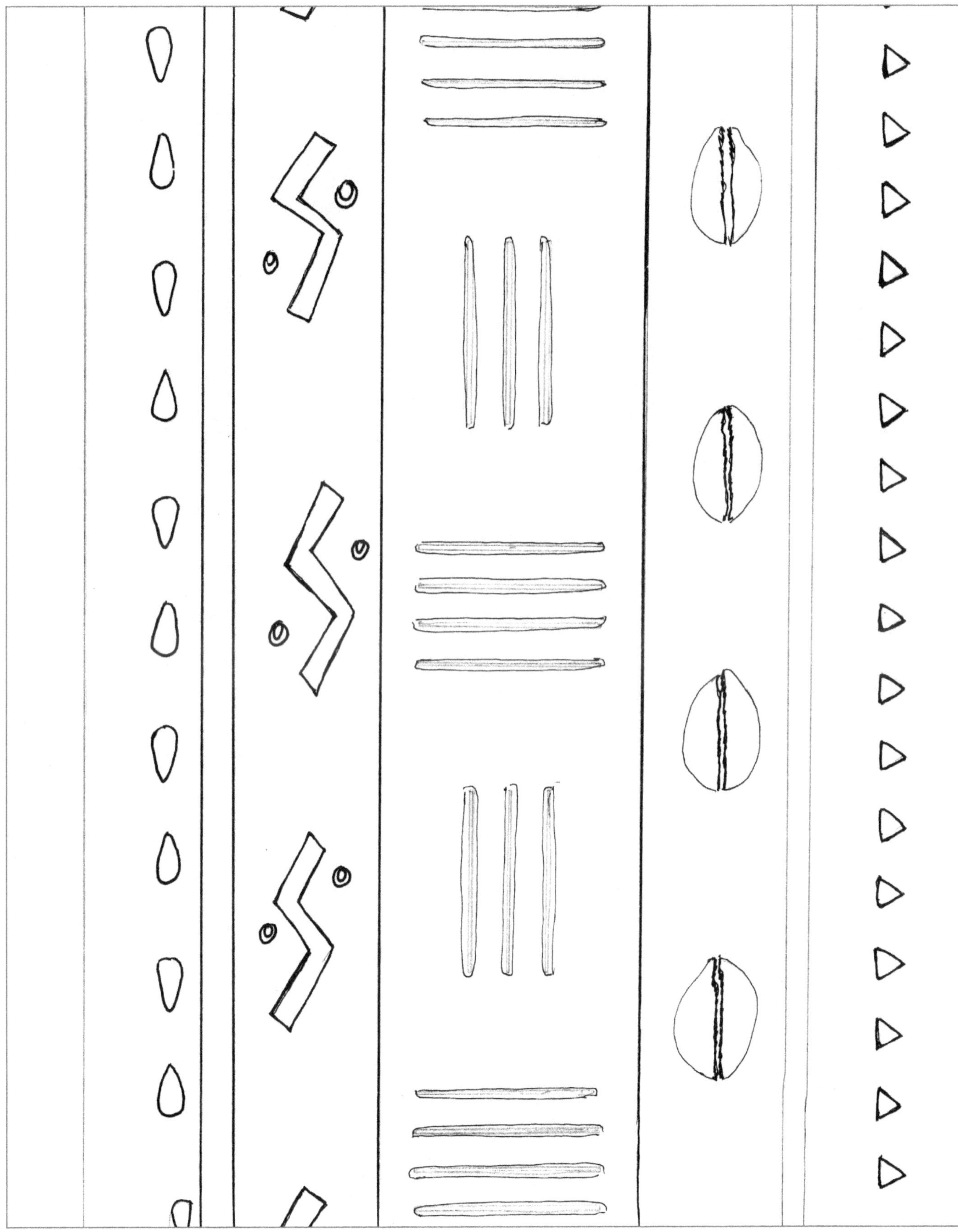

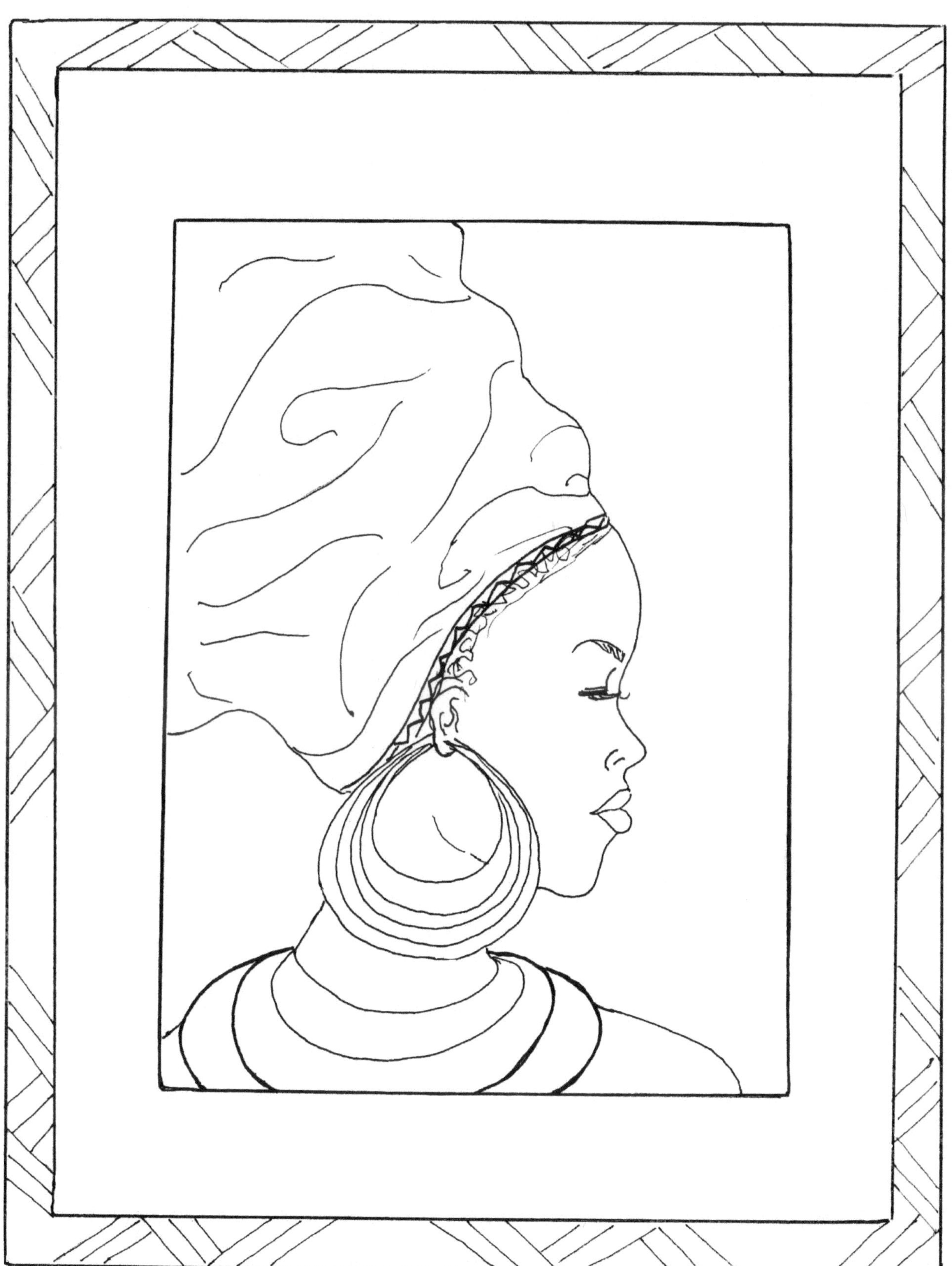

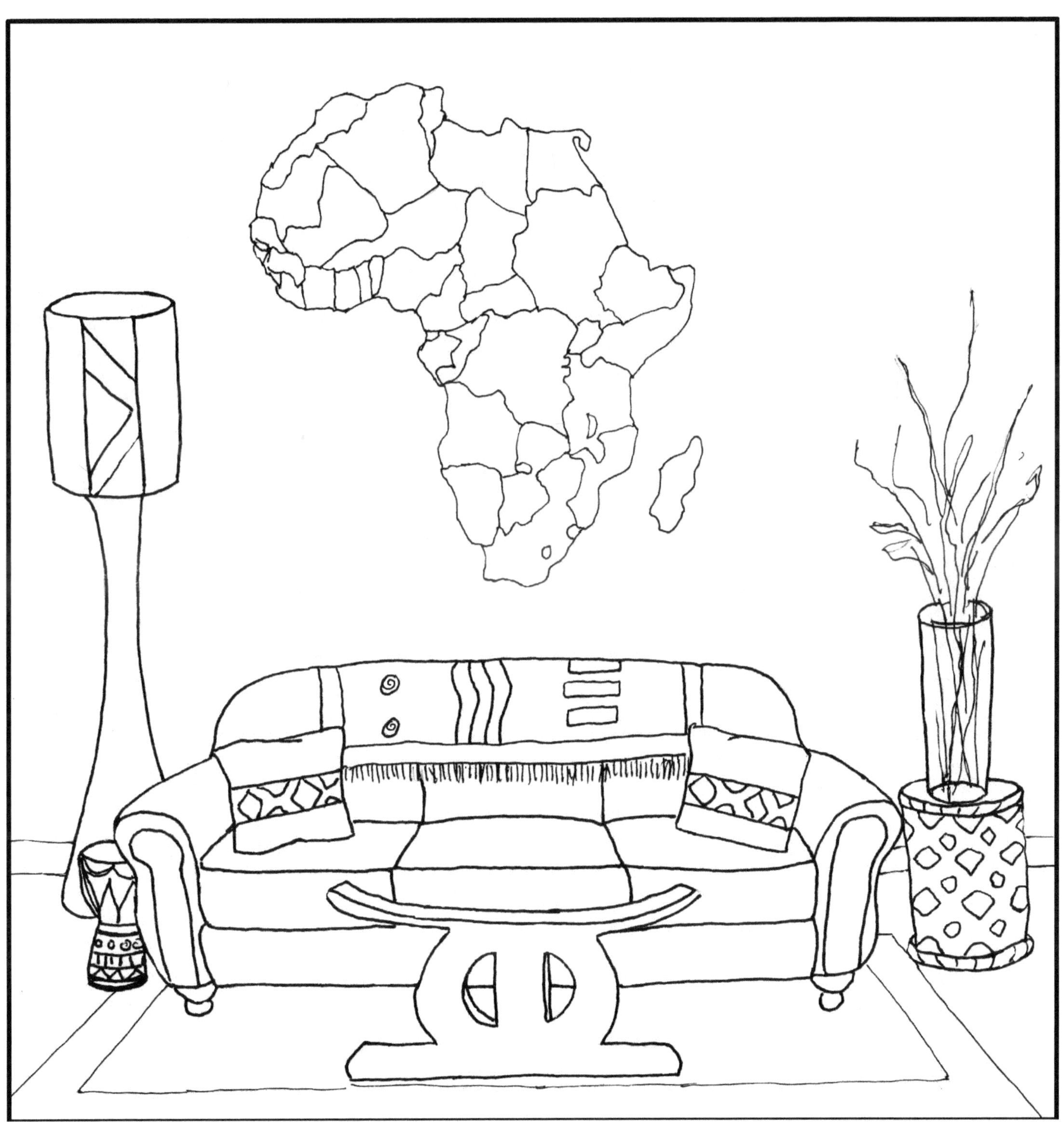

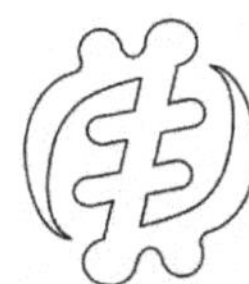

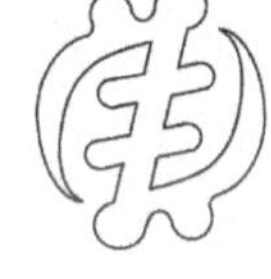

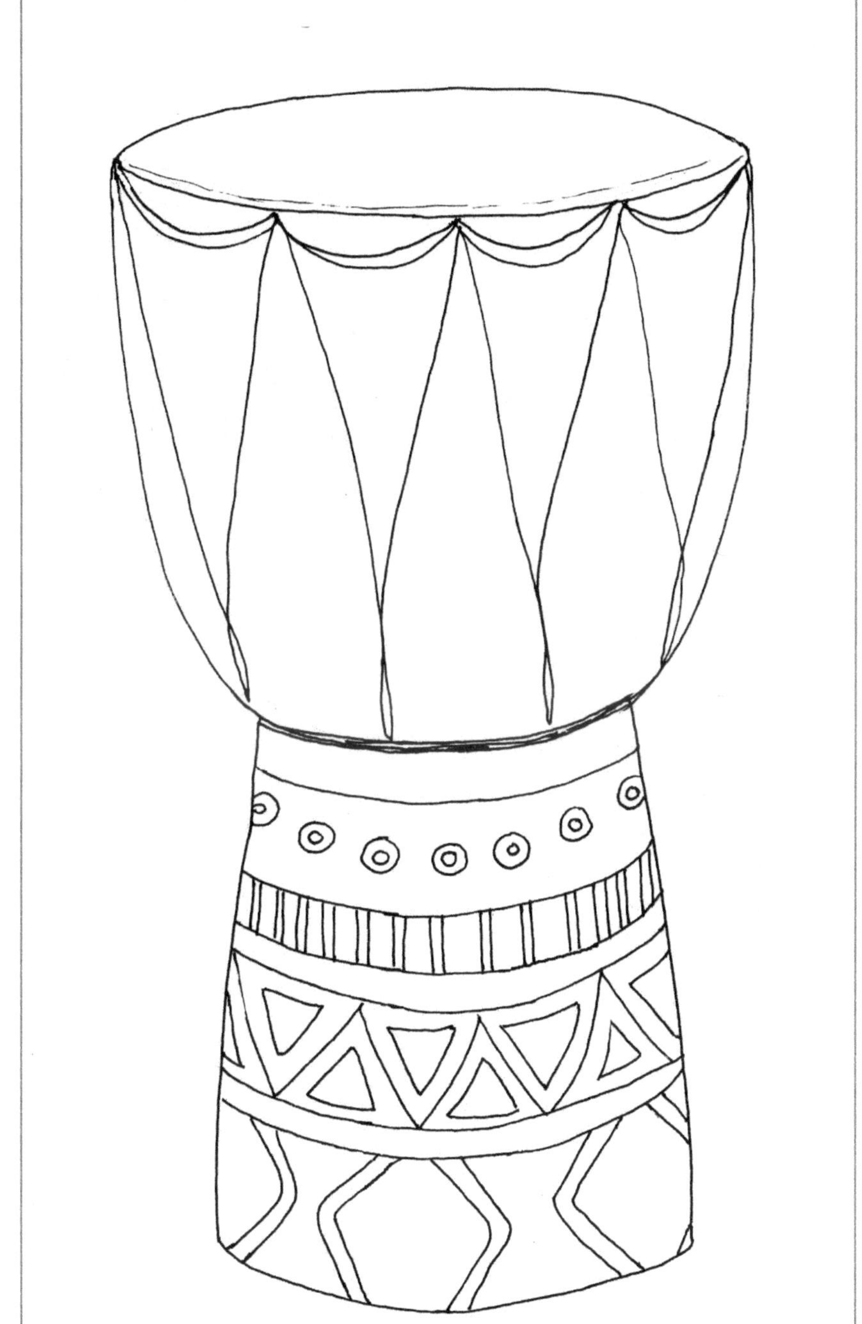

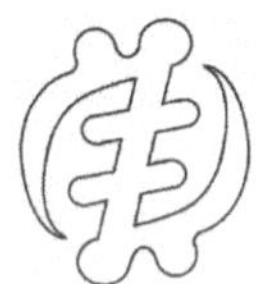

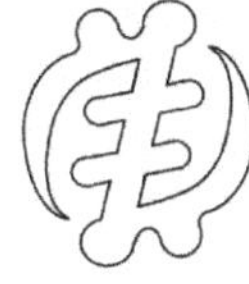

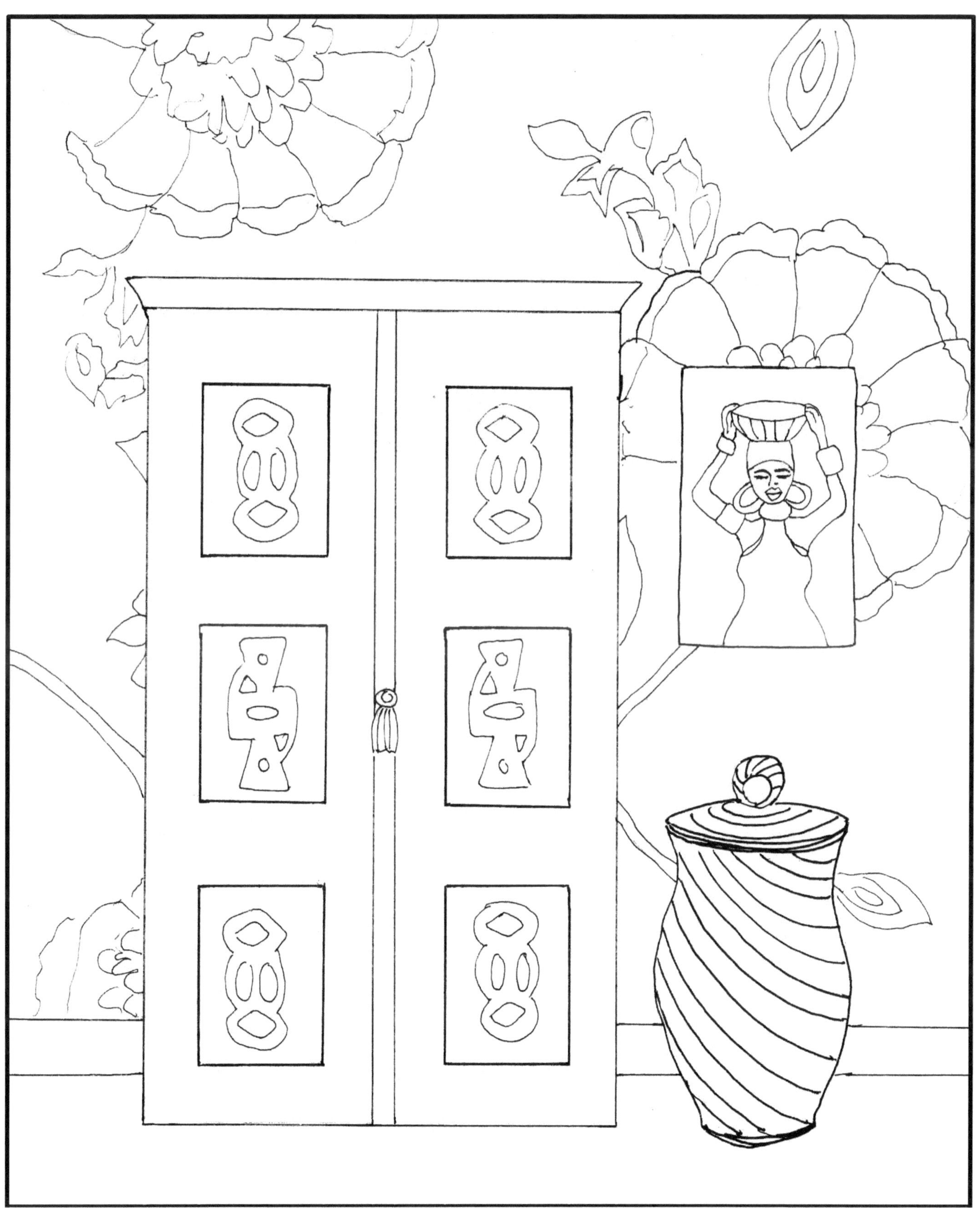

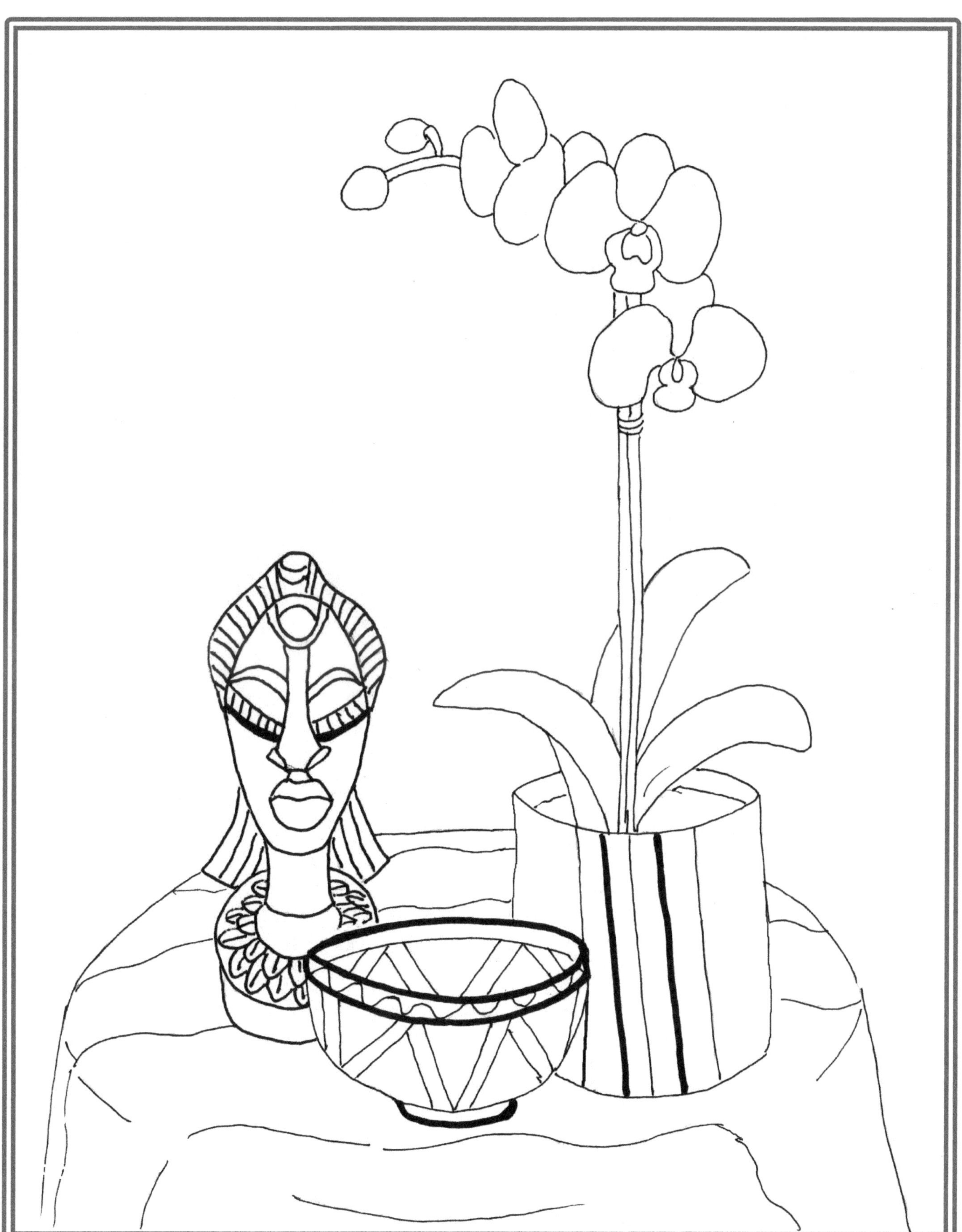

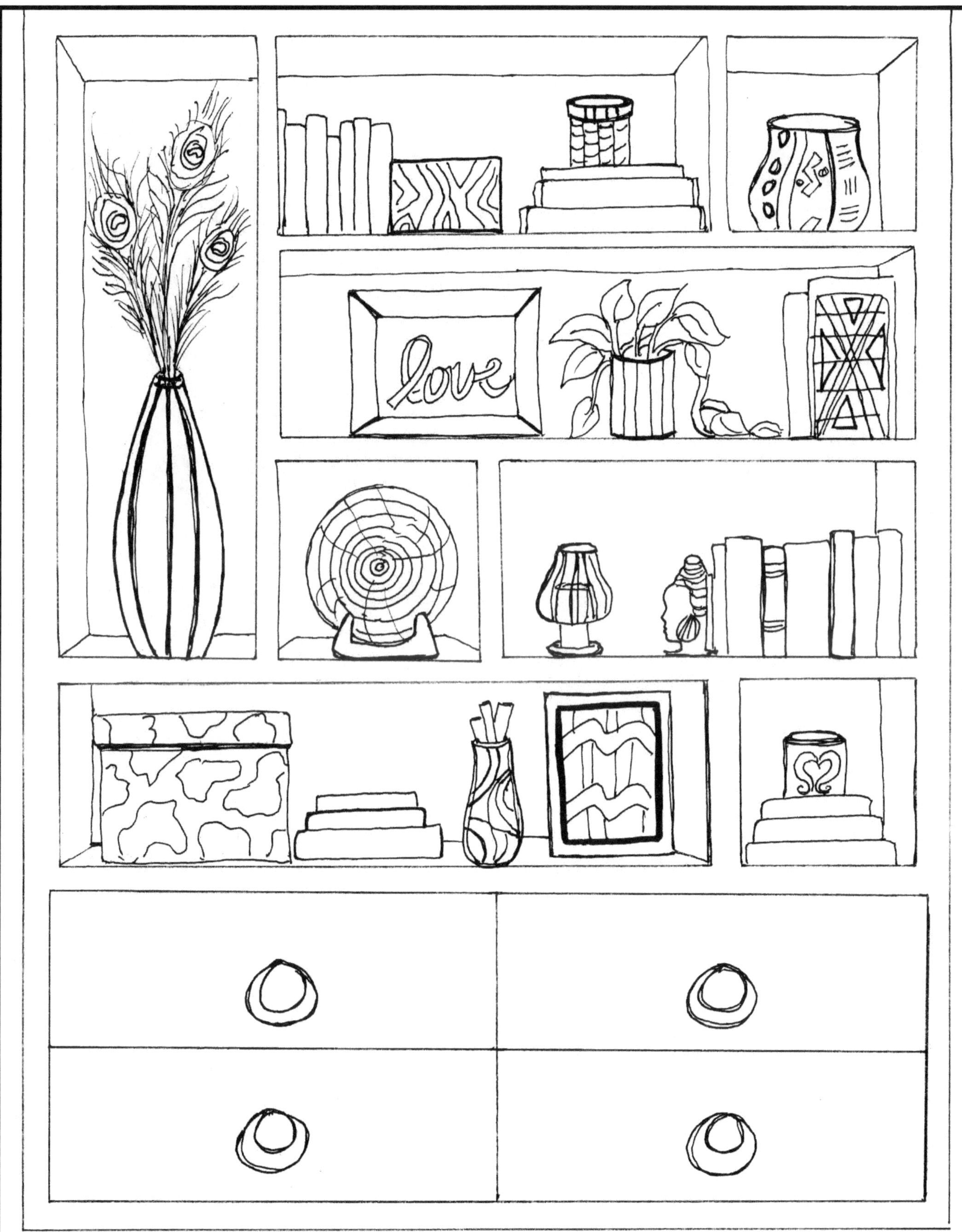
love

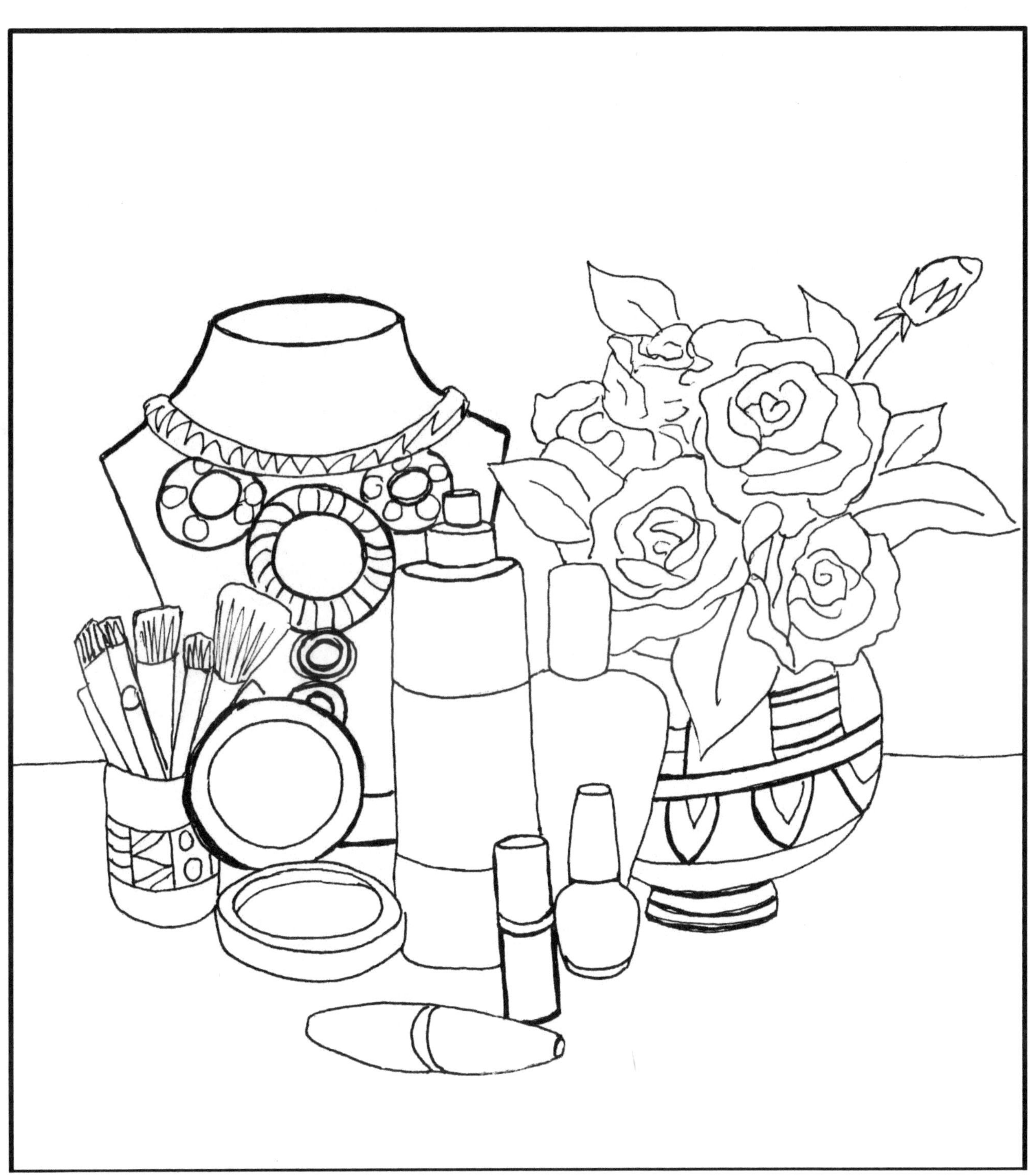

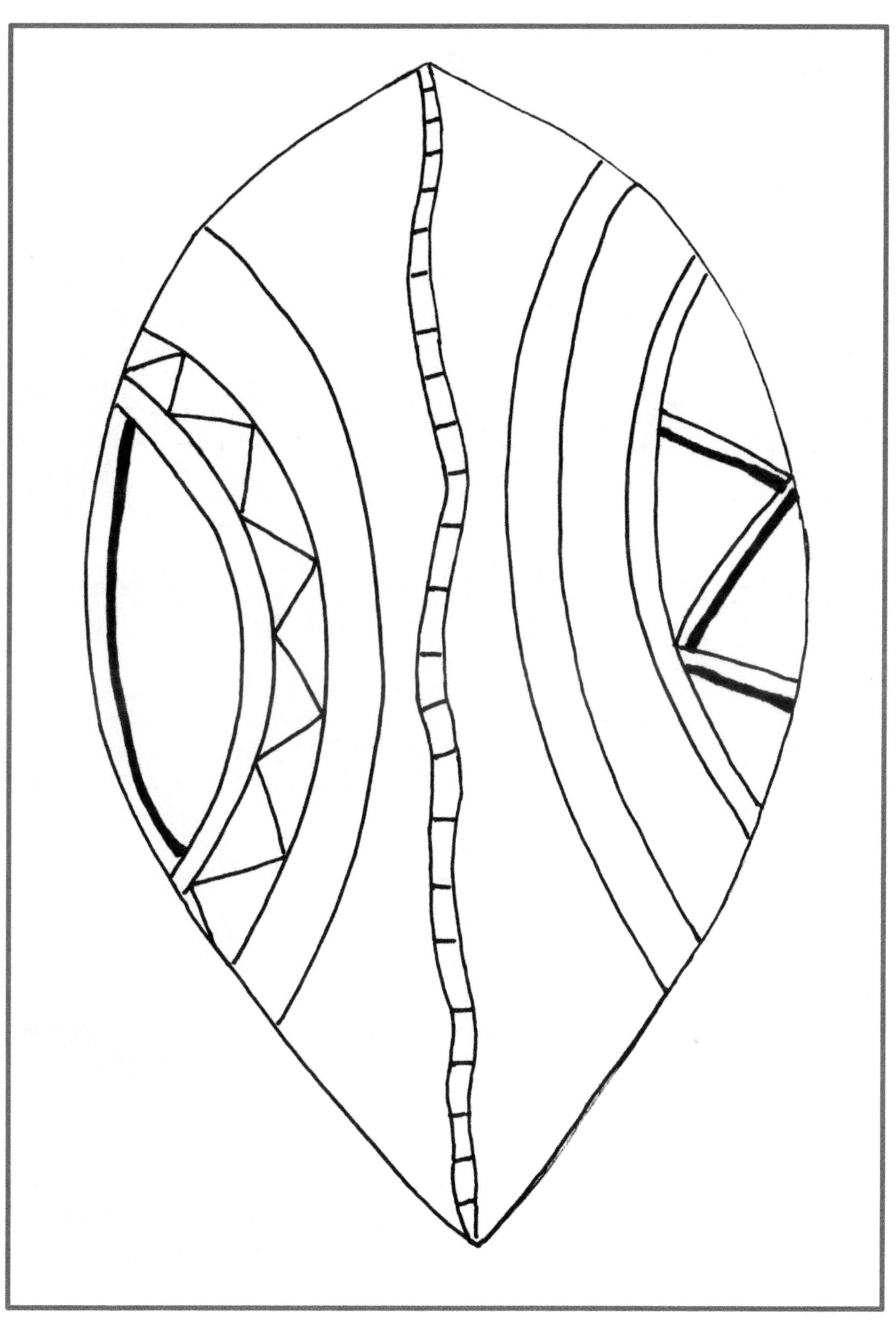

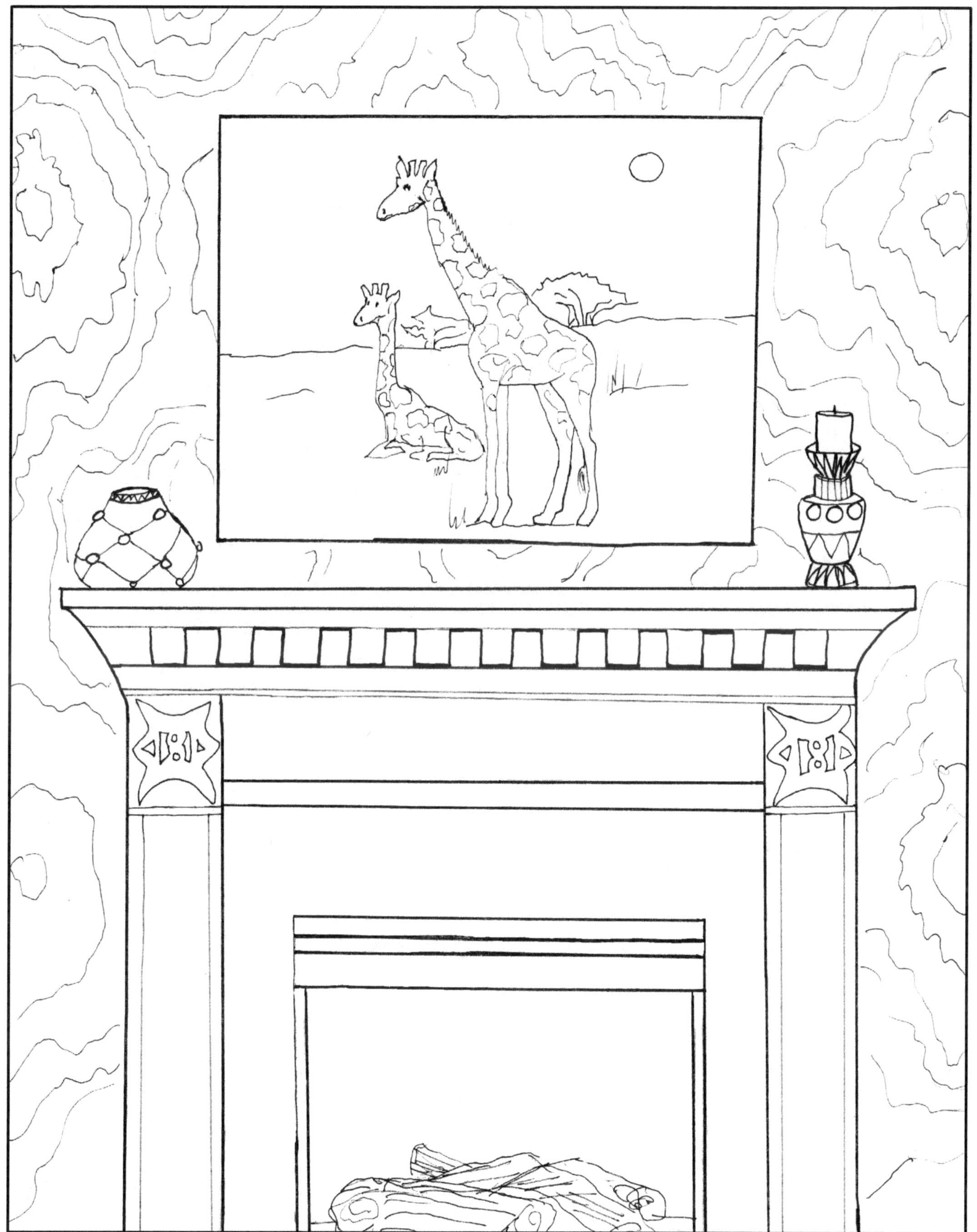

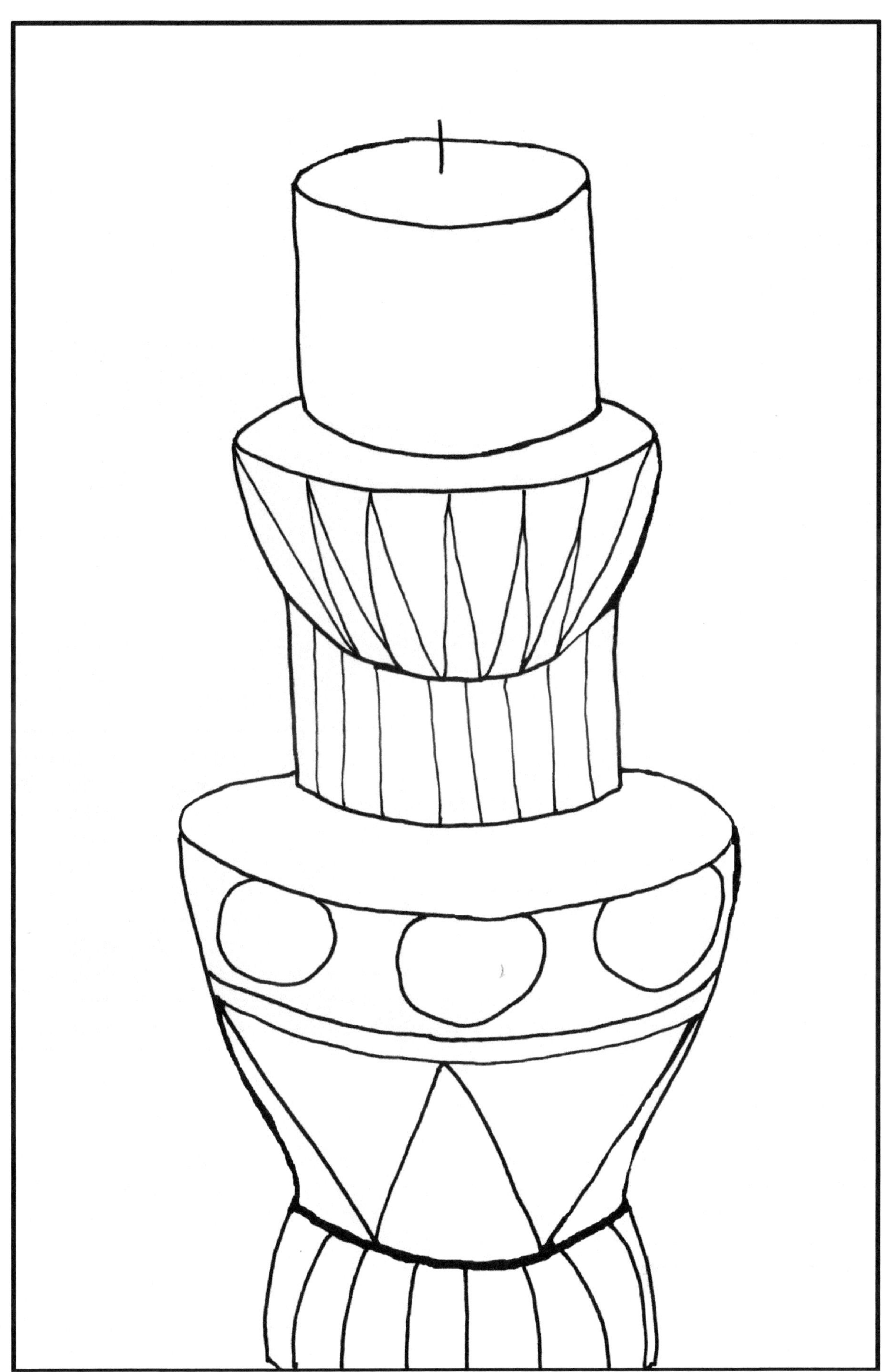

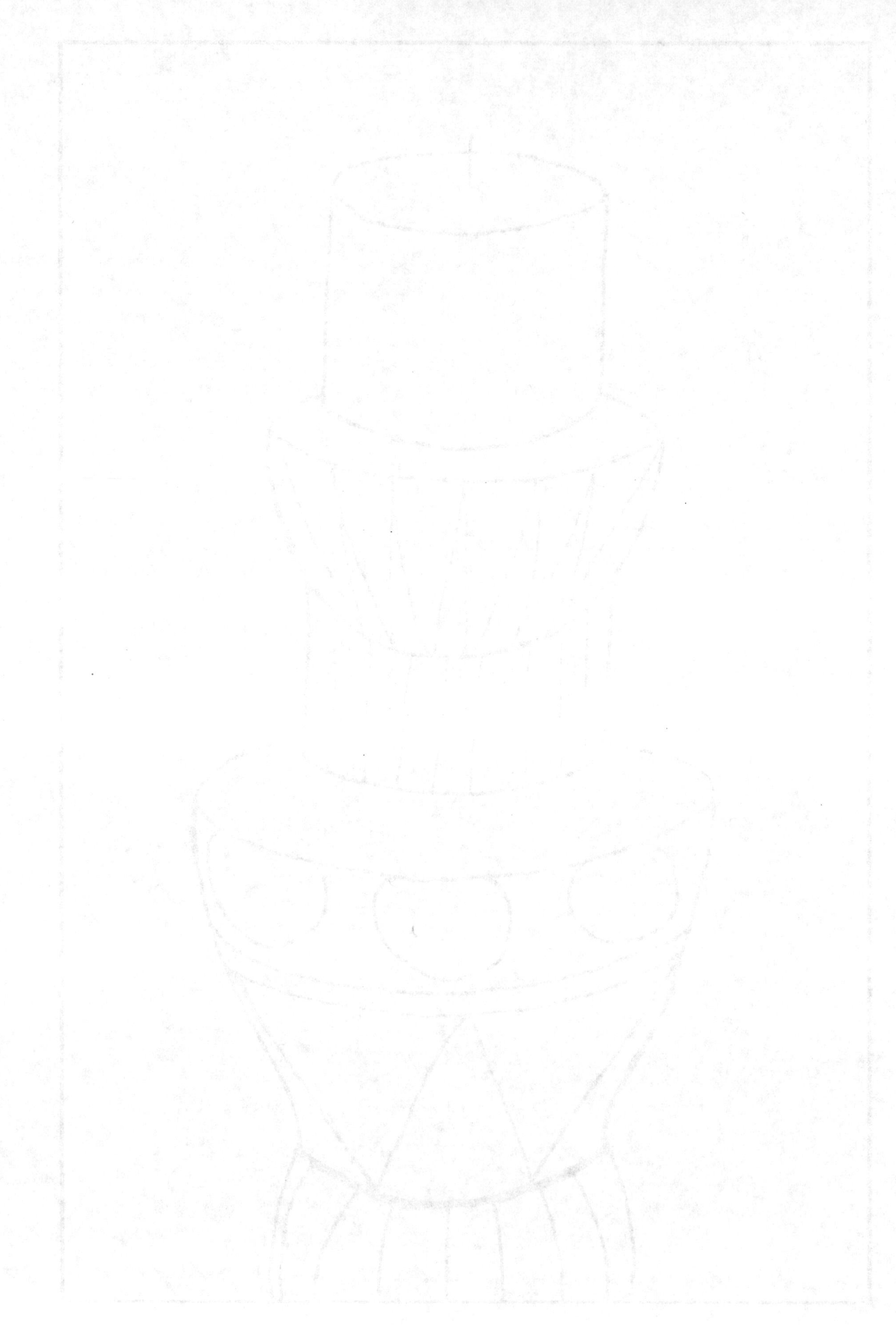

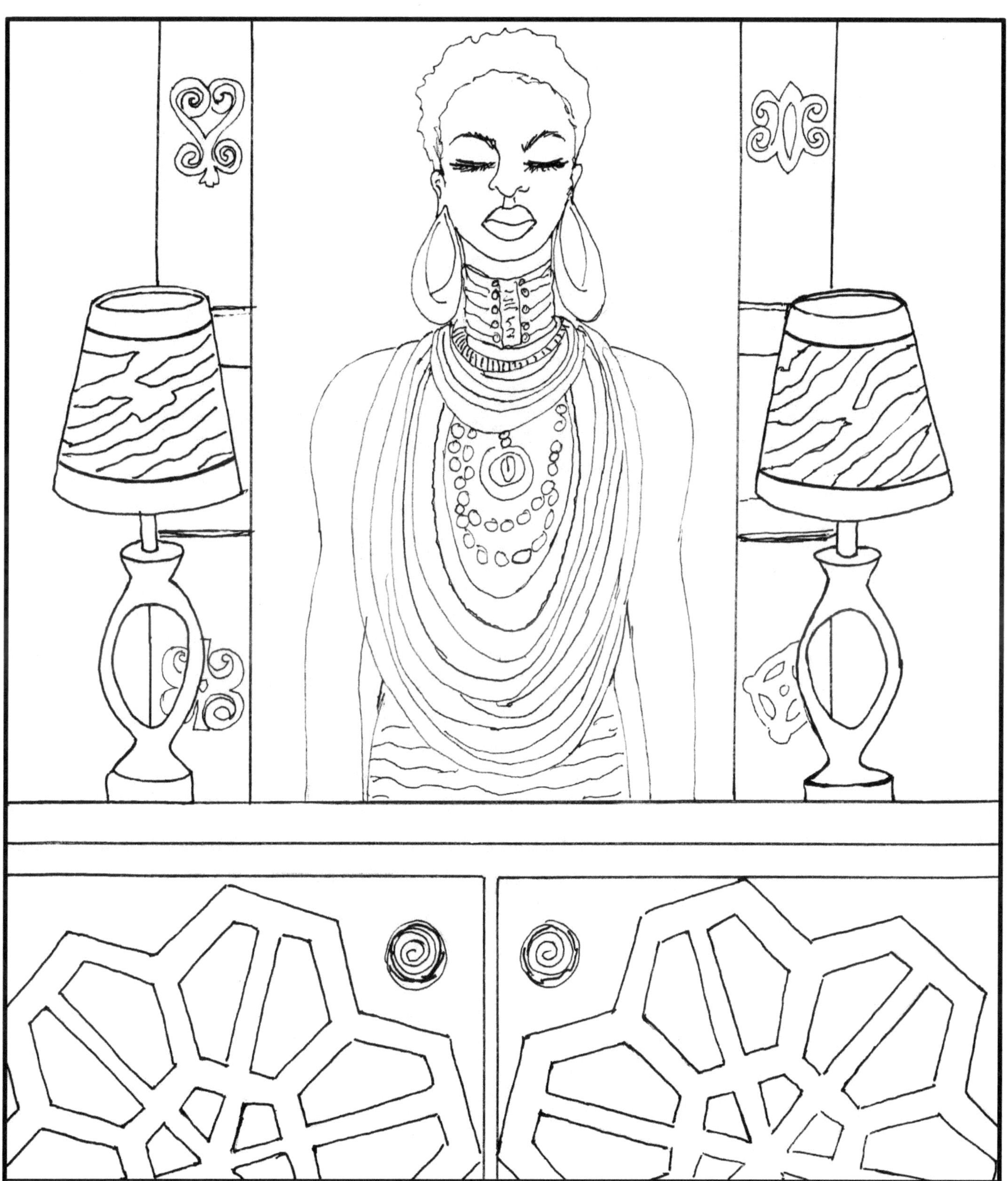

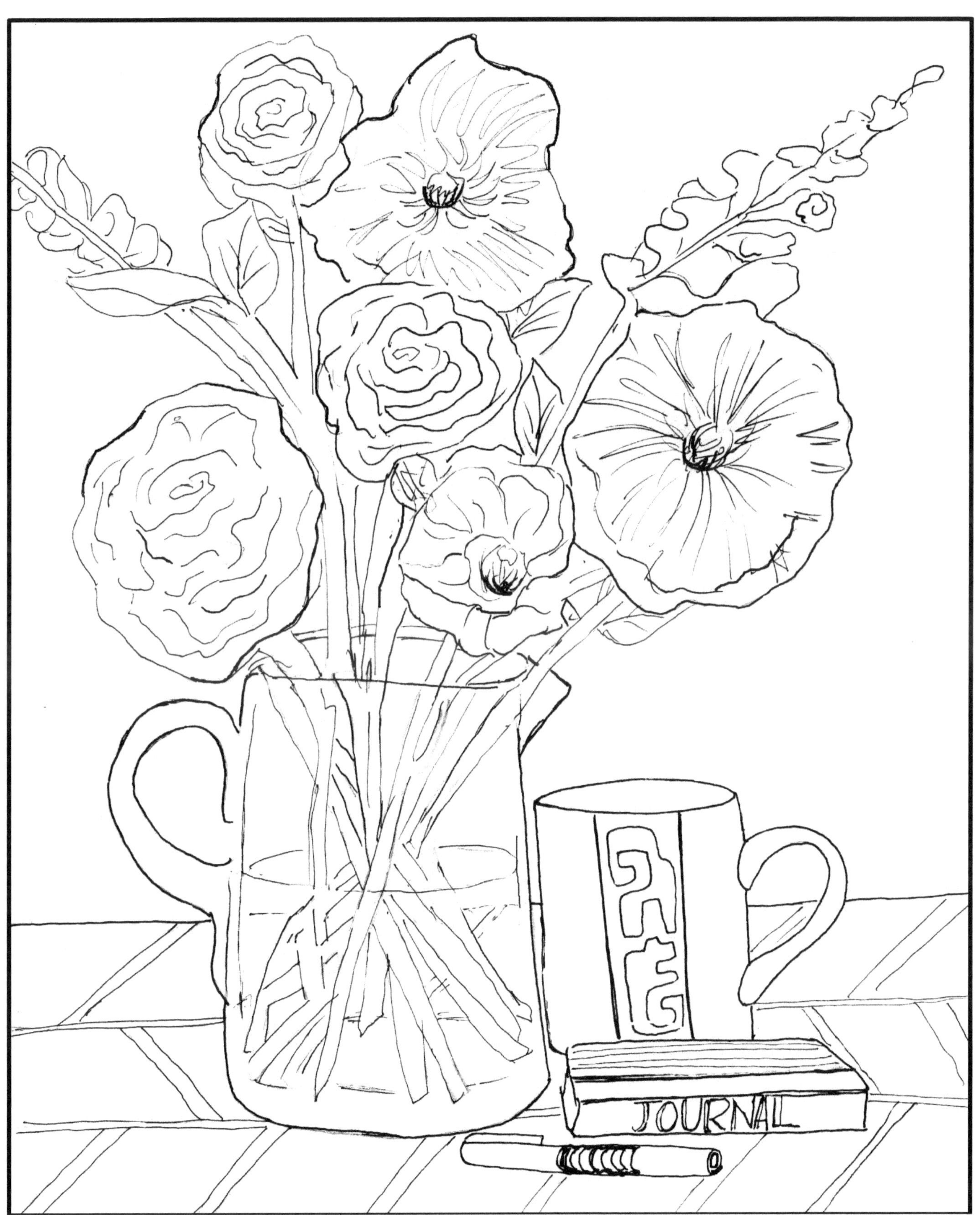
JOURNAL

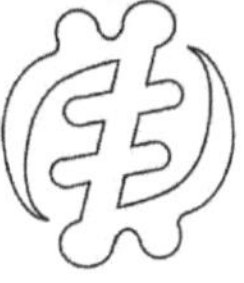

believe

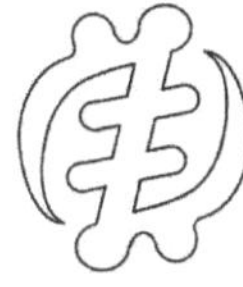

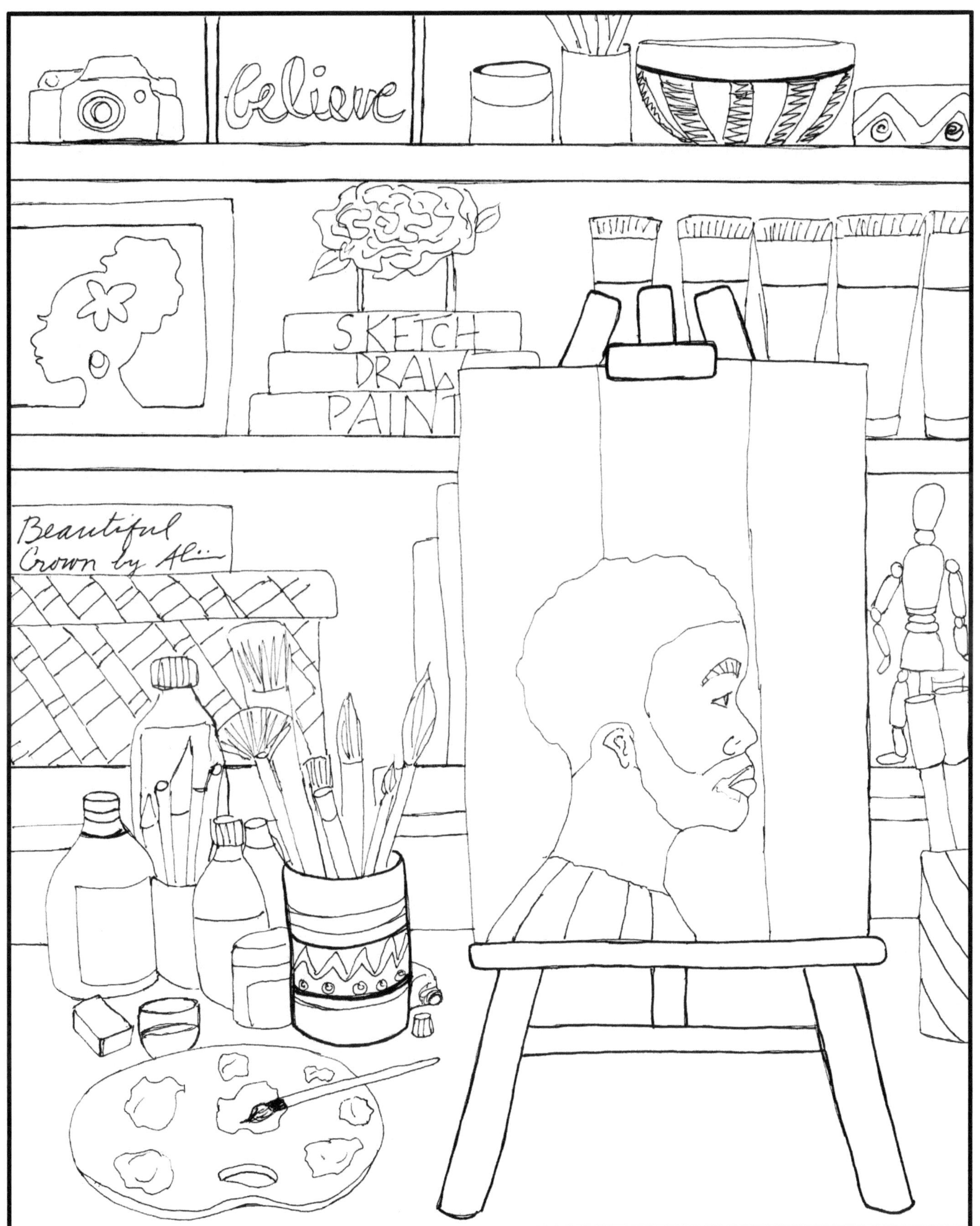
believe
SKETCH
DRAW
PAINT
Beautiful
Crown by

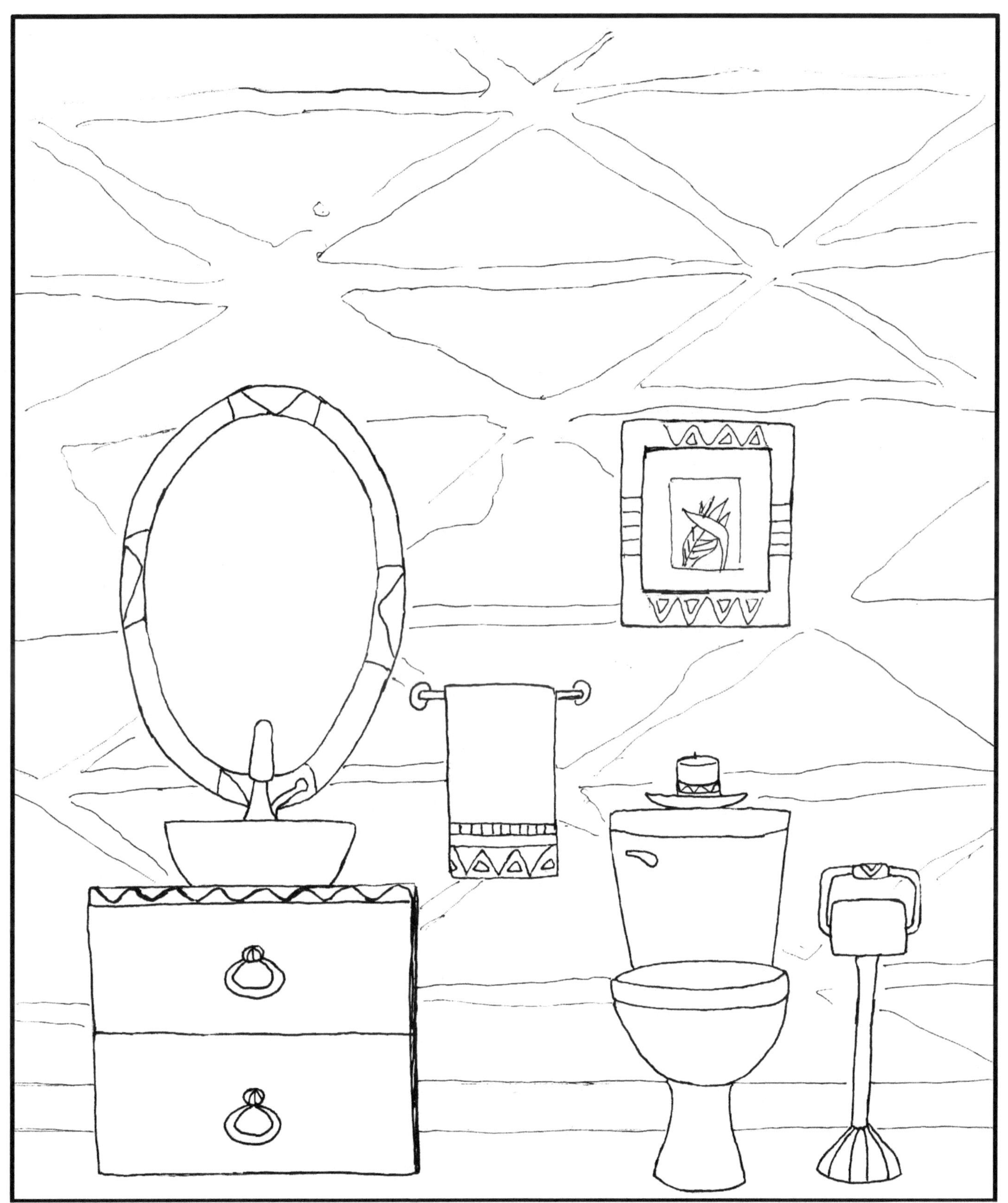

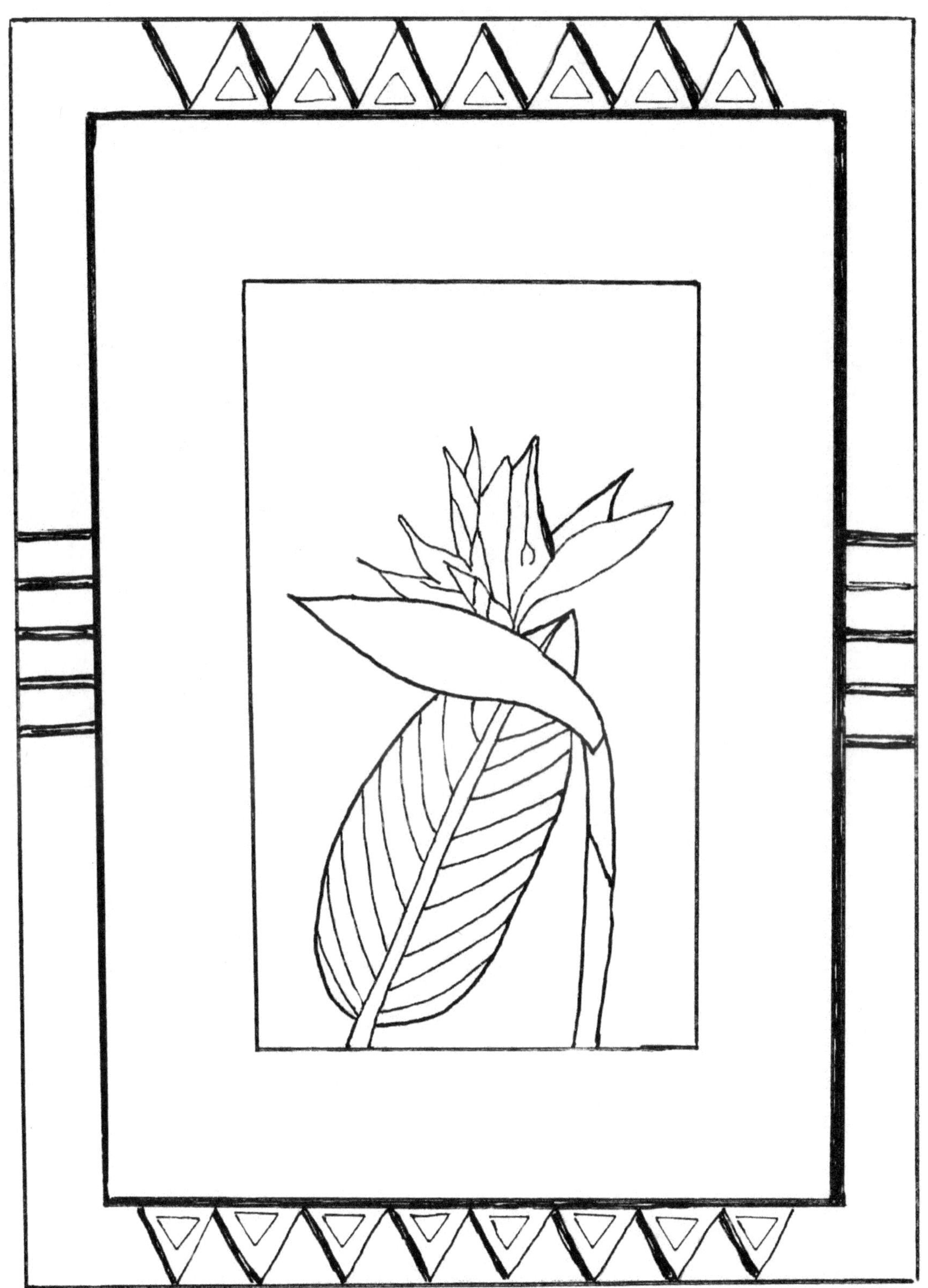

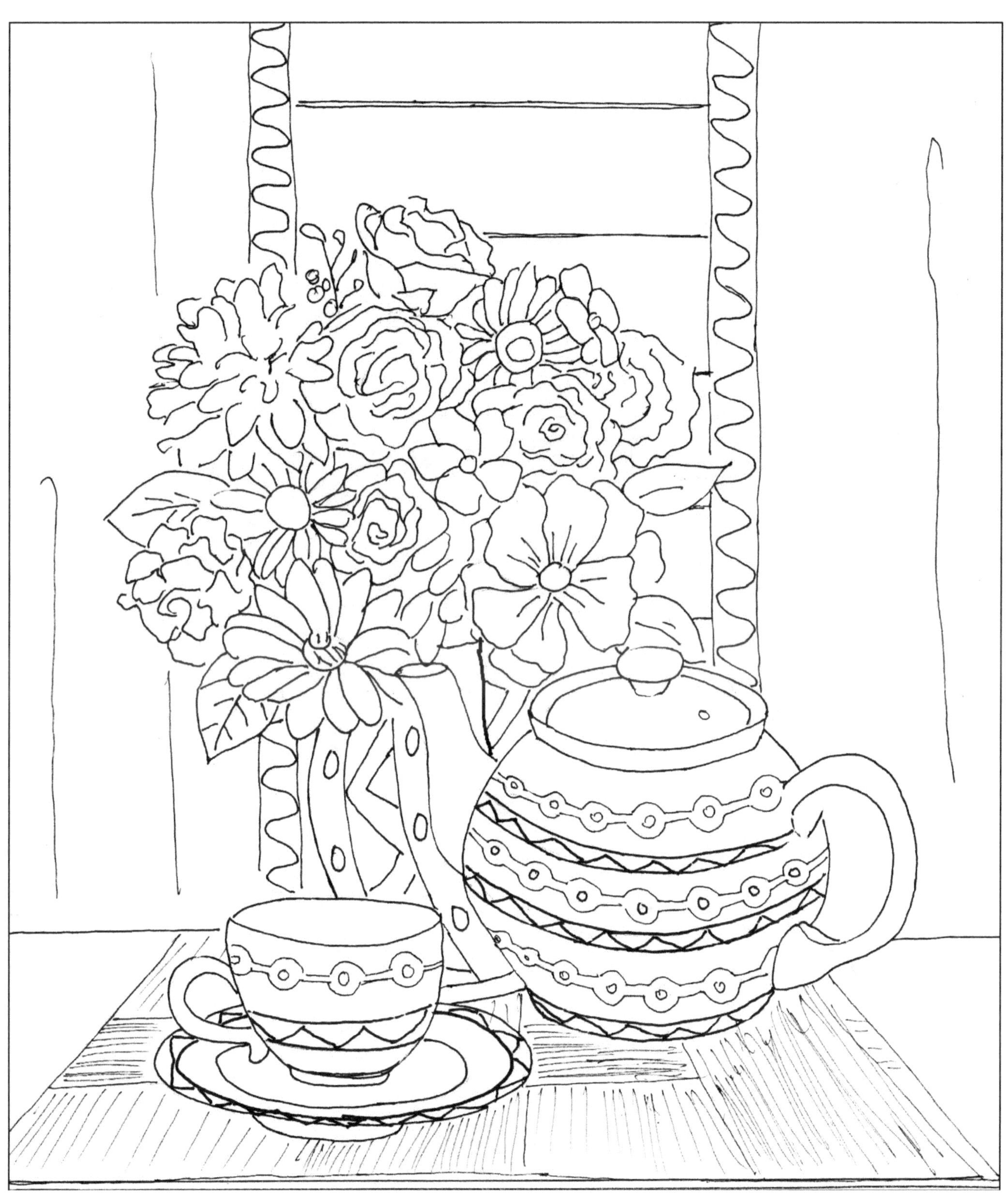

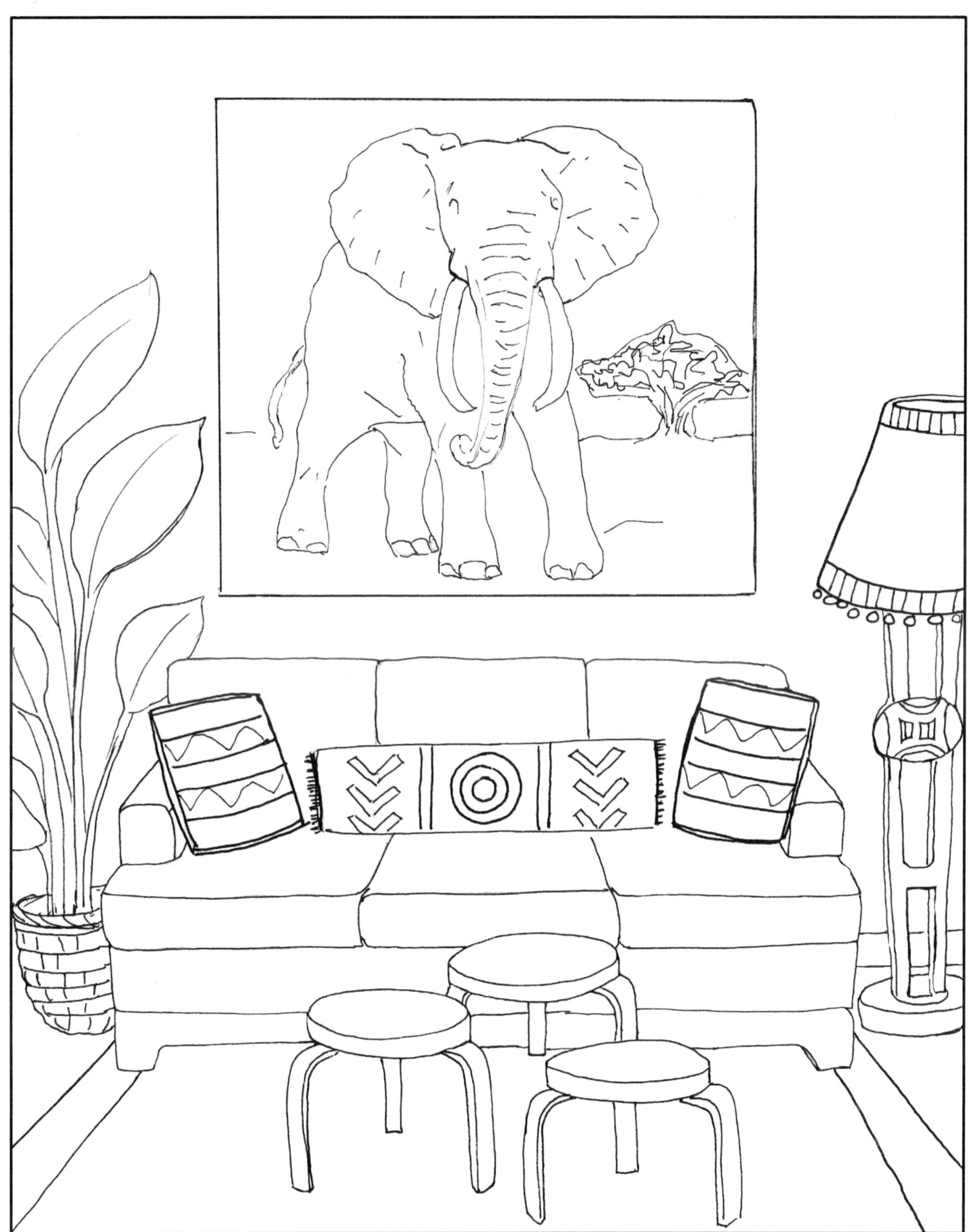

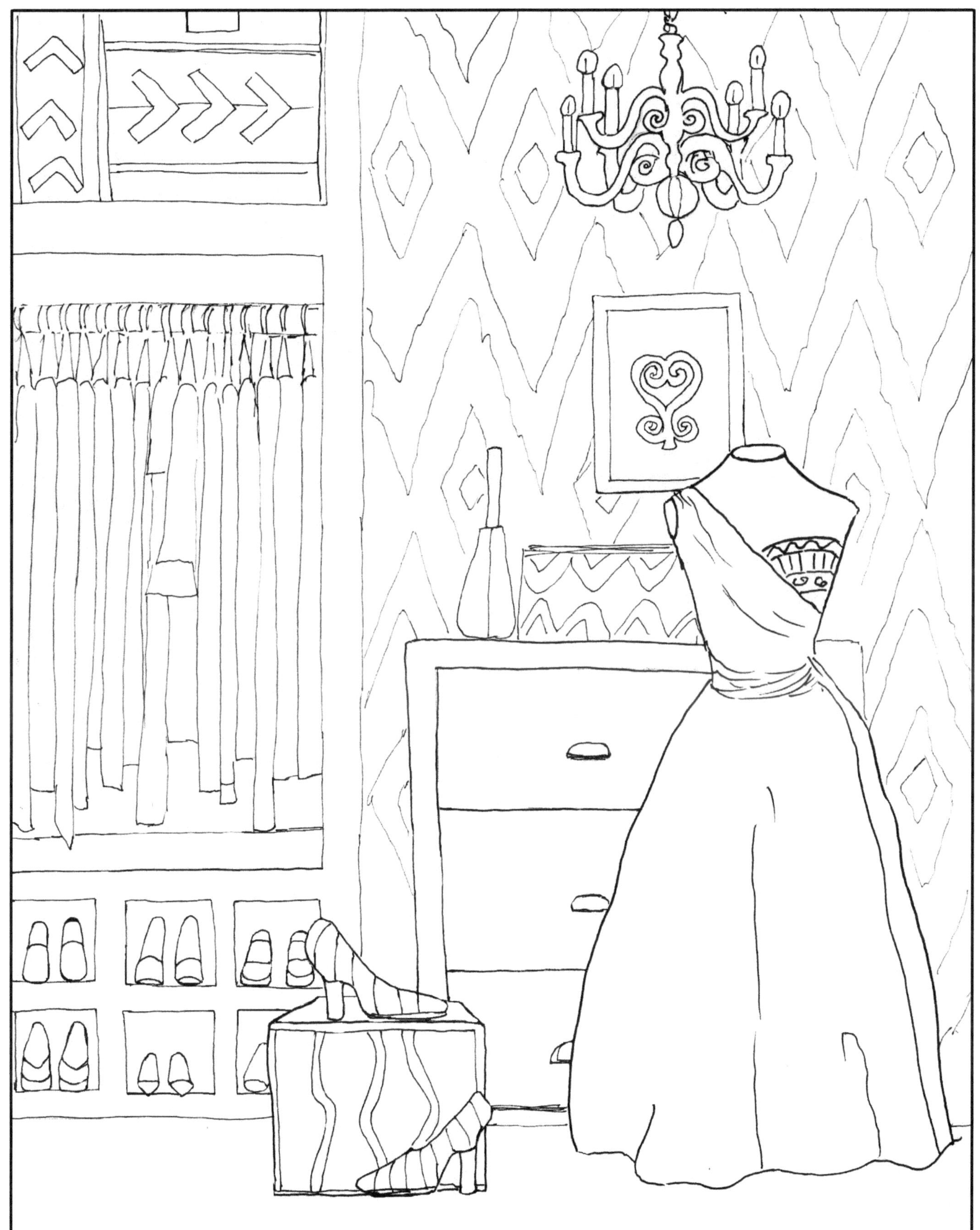

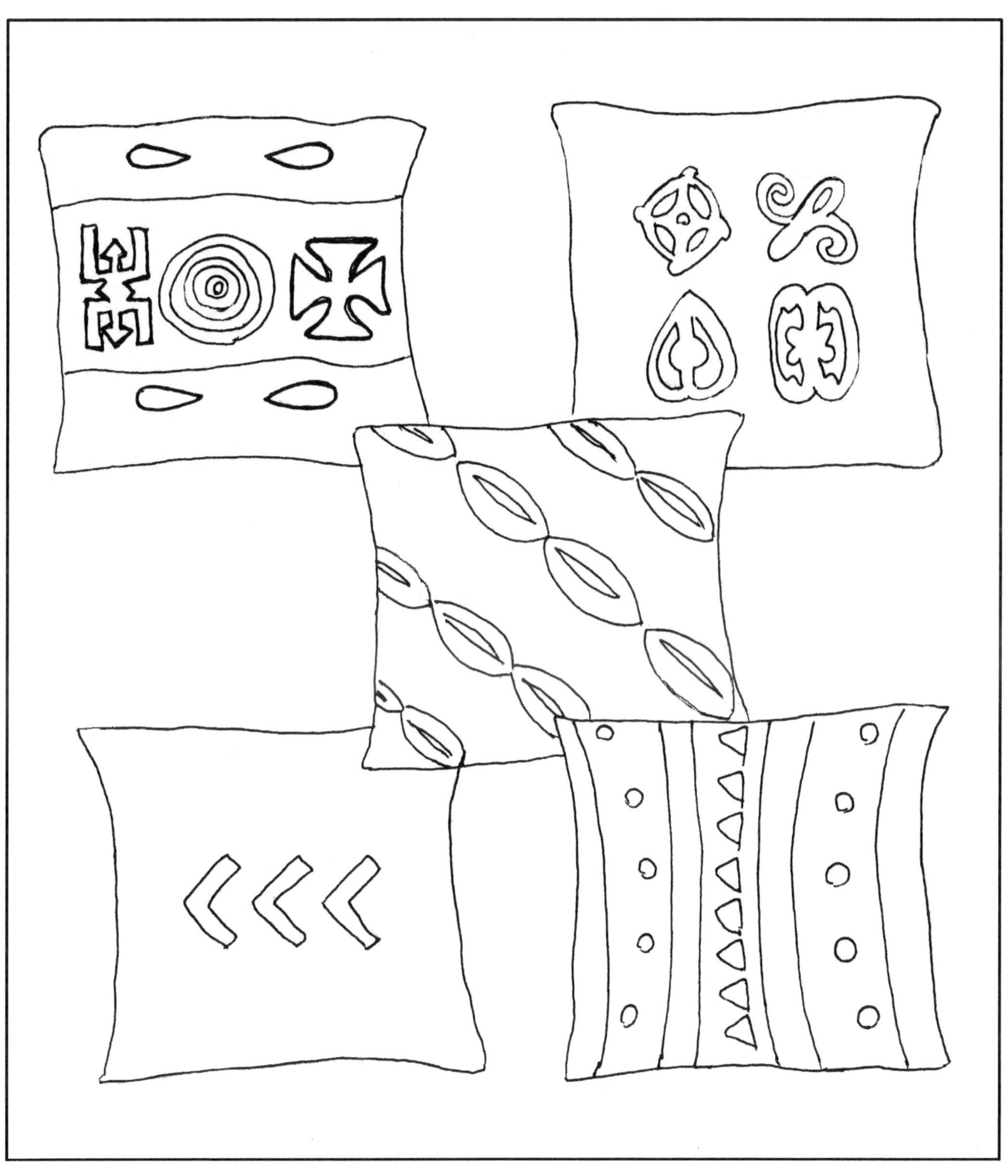

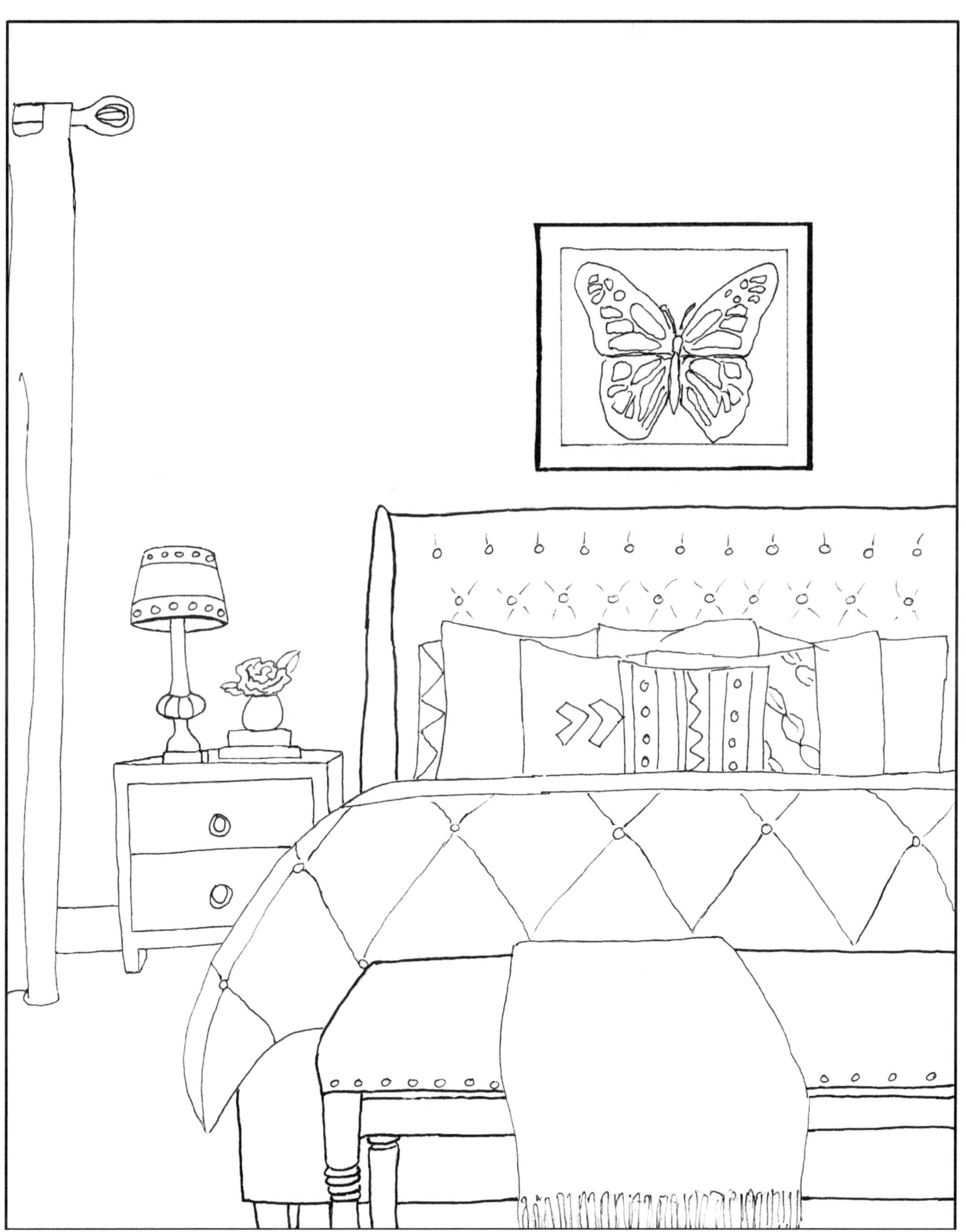

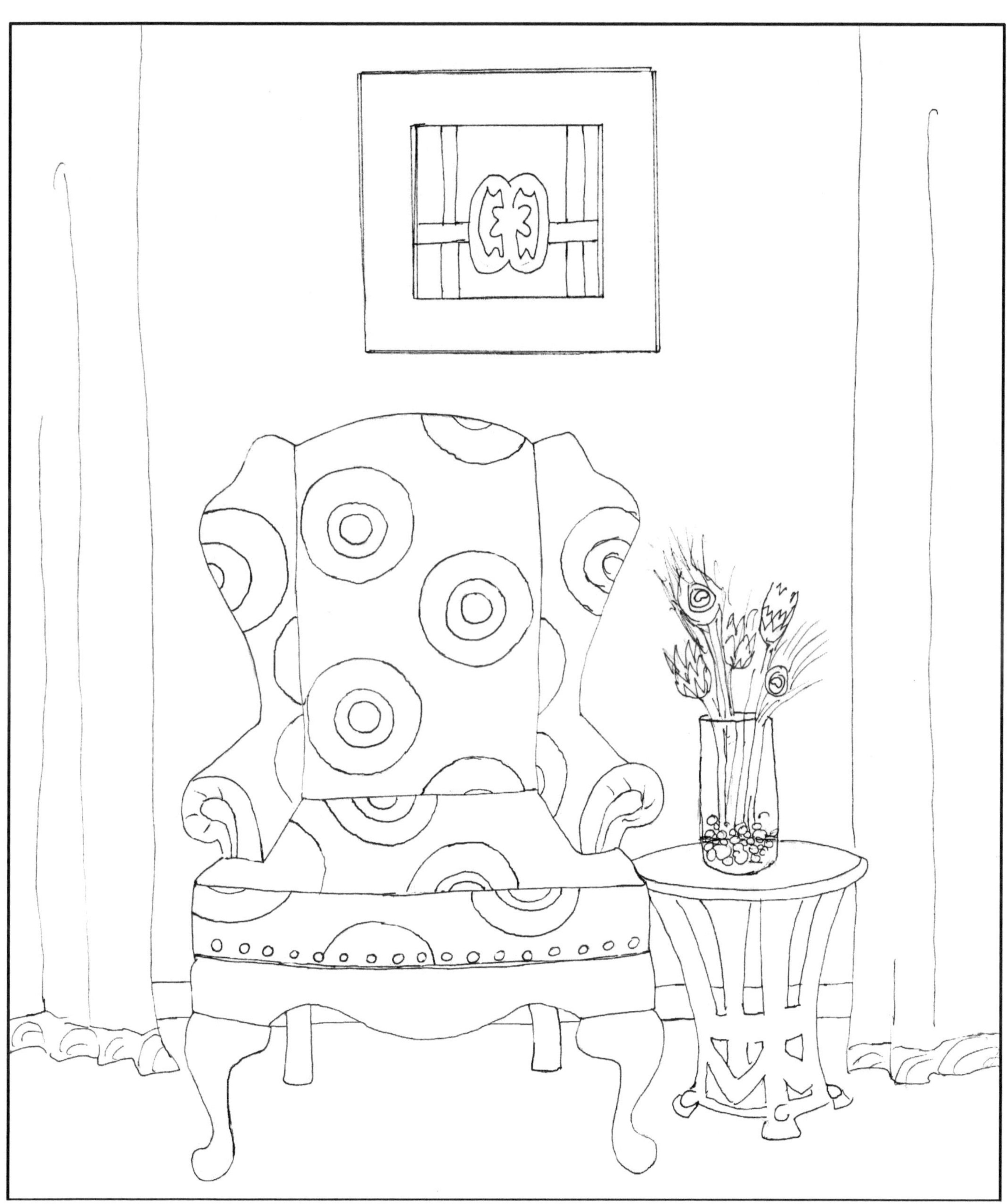

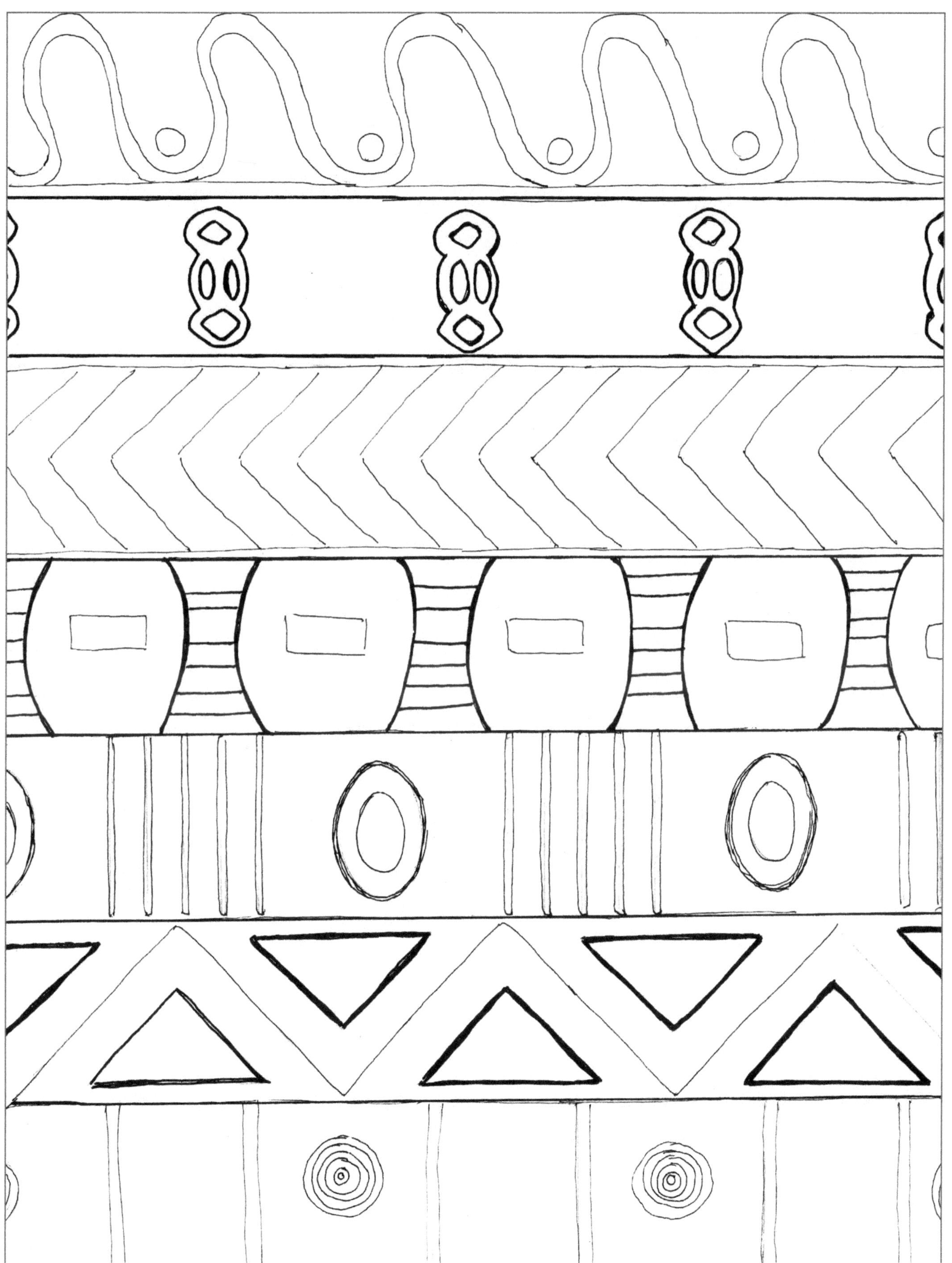

Test Color Page

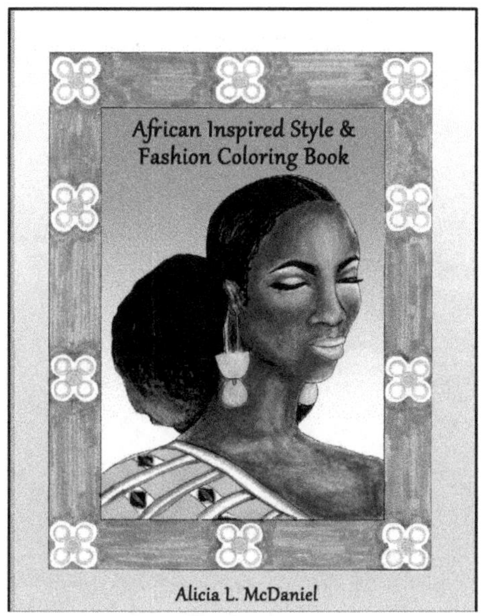
African Inspired Style &
Fashion Coloring Book
Alicia L. McDaniel

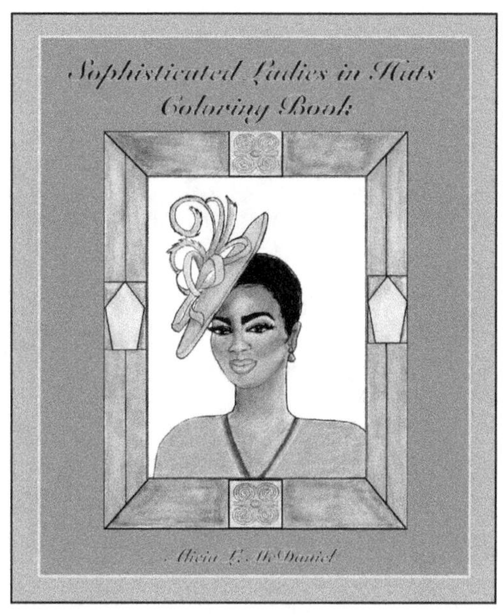
Sophisticated Ladies in Hats
Coloring Book

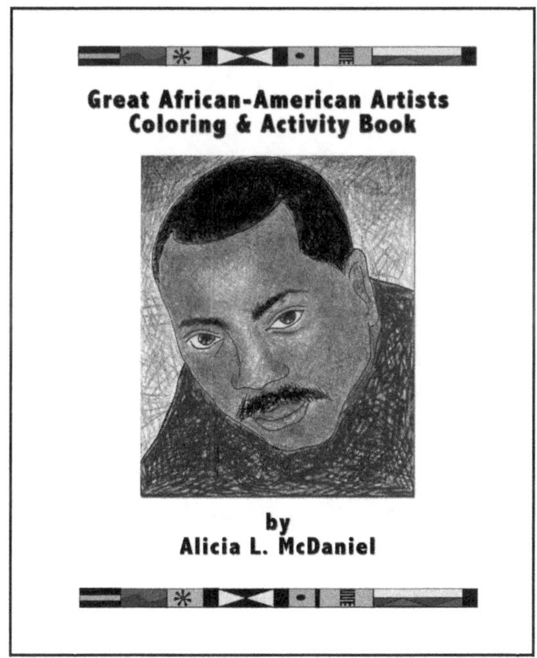
Great African-American Artists
Coloring & Activity Book
by
Alicia L. McDaniel

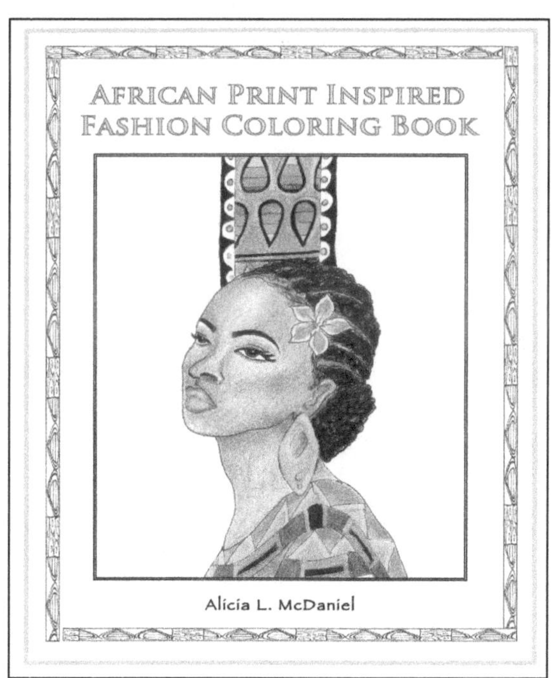
AFRICAN PRINT INSPIRED
FASHION COLORING BOOK
Alicia L. McDaniel

www.ingramcontent.com/pod-product-compliance
Lightning Source LLC
LaVergne TN
LVHW081423110826
845149LV00010B/1848
9780999557334